NOTE TO PARENTS

Welcome to Kingfisher Readers! This program is designed to help young readers build skills, confidence, and a love of reading as they explore their favorite topics.

These tips can help you get more from the experience of reading books together. But remember, the most important thing is to make reading fun!

Tips to Warm Up Before Reading

- Look through the book with your child. Ask them what they notice about the pictures.
- Wonder aloud together. Ask questions and make predictions. What will this book be about? What are some words we could expect to find on these pages?

While Reading

- Take turns or read together until your child takes over.
- Point to the words as you say them.
- When your child gets stuck on a word, ask if the picture could help. Then think about the first letter too.
- Accept and praise your child's contributions.

After Reading

- Look back at the things your child found interesting. Encourage connections to other things you both know.
- Draw pictures or make models to explore these ideas.
- Read the book again soon, to build fluency.

With five distinct levels and a wealth of appealing topics, the Kingfisher Readers series provides children with an exciting way to learn to read about the world around them. Enjoy!

Ellie Costa, M.S. Ed.
Literacy Specialist, Bank Street School for Children, New York

KINGFISHER
READERS

level
1

Animal Colors

Thea Feldman

KINGFISHER
NEW YORK

KINGFISHER
LONDON & NEW YORK

Copyright © Kingfisher 2014
Published in the United States and Canada by Kingfisher,
175 Fifth Ave., New York, NY 10010
Kingfisher is an imprint of Macmillan Children's Books, London.
All rights reserved.

Distributed in the U.S. by Macmillan,
175 Fifth Ave., New York, NY 10010

Library of Congress Cataloging-in-Publication data
has been applied for.

Series editor: Thea Feldman
Literacy consultant: Ellie Costa, Bank Street School for Children, New York

978-0-7534-7134-0 (HB)
978-0-7534-7135-7 (PB)

Kingfisher books are available for special promotions
and premiums. For details contact: Special Markets
Department, Macmillan, 175 Fifth Ave.,
New York, NY 10010.

For more information, please visit
www.kingfisherbooks.com

Printed in China
9 8 7 6 5 4 3 2 1
1TR/0713/WKT/UG/115MA

Picture credits
The Publisher would like to thank the following for permission to reproduce their
material. Every care has been taken to trace copyright holders. However, if there
have been unintentional omissions or failure to trace copyright holders, we apologize
and will, if informed, endeavor to make corrections in any future edition.

Top = t; Bottom = b; Center = c; Left = l; Right = r
Cover Steve Parish/Steve Parish Publishing/Corbis; 3 Shutterstock/chrom; 4 FLPA/Piotr Naskrecki/
Minden Pictures; 5 Shutterstock/Yellowj; 6t FLPA/Ingo Arndt/Minden Pictures;
6b Shutterstock; 7t; FLPA/moomsabuy; 7b FLPA/Fabio Pupin; 8 FLPA/Michael Breuer/Biosphoto;
9 Shutterstock/Neale Cousland; 10t Shutterstock/Jason S.; 10b Shutterstock/Mogens Trolle;
11t Shutterstock/Hung Chung Chih; 11b FLPA/Norbert Probst/Imagebroker; 12l Shutterstock/
Serg64; 12r Shutterstock/Eric Isselee; 13t Shutterstock/Khoroshunova Olga; 13b Shutterstock/Eric
Isselee; 14l Shutterstock/ romanvm66; 14c Shutterstock/Eric Isselee; 15t Shutterstock/bmaki;
15b Shutterstock/stockshotportfolio; 16–17 FLPA/Alfred Schauhuber/Imagebroker;
18 Shutterstock/Eduard Kyslynskyy; 19 FLPA/Bernd Rohrschneider; 20 Shutterstock/Ian Grainger;
21 Shutterstock/Sue Robinson; 22 FLPA/Bernd Rohrschneider; 23 FLPA/Thorsten Negro/
Imagebroker; 24t Shutterstock/Alfredo Maiquez; 24b Shutterstock/ Kletr; 25t Shutterstock/Brandon
Alms; 25b Shutterstock/Dirk Ercken; 26 Shutterstock/Steve McWilliam; 27 Shutterstock/James
Coleman; 28 FLPA/Thomas Marent/Minden Pictures; 29 Shutterstock/apiguide; 30t Shutterstock/
worldswildlifewonders; 30bl FLPA/GTW/Imagebroker; 31t Shutterstock/Dobermaraner;
31b Shutterstock/Marty Wakat.

There are many colorful
animals in the world!

This grasshopper
is bright green.

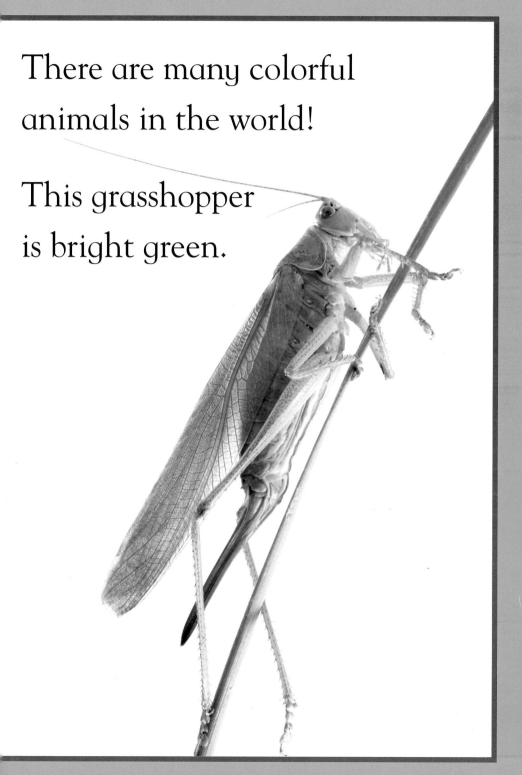

This snake is green too.

These birds are pink.

This crab is red.

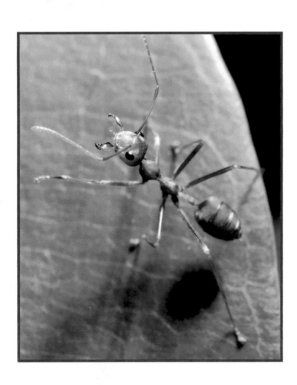

So is
this ant.

This sea star
is blue.

So is this lizard.

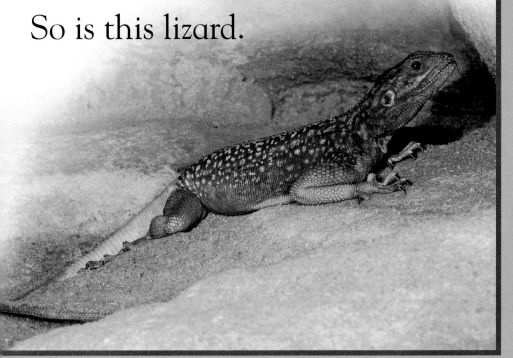

This bear is brown
from its head to its tail.

It is all one color.

Some animals are
more than one color.

How many different
colors do you see
on this bird?

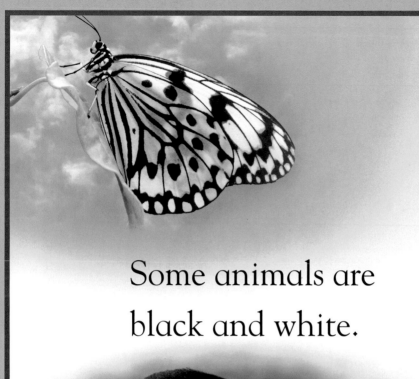

Some animals are
black and white.

11

Some animals
have spots.

Some animals
have stripes.

The colors of some animals
help them hide
from other animals.

This is called **camouflage**
(say CAM-uh-flahj).

This brown **hare** hides
from animals that hunt.

Its fur helps the hare
blend in with the grass
and the ground.

Do you see it?

A tiger is a hunter.

It has black and orange stripes.

A tiger's stripes help it
hide in tall grass.

The tiger hides until
an animal comes near.

Then the tiger will jump
out to catch it!

Some animals change
their colors!

This spider is white
when it is on a white flower.

It turns yellow on a
yellow flower.

Insects do not see the spider.

The spider grabs and eats
this insect!

Sometimes this chameleon
(say ka-MEE-lee-yun)
is green.

Now it is red and white!

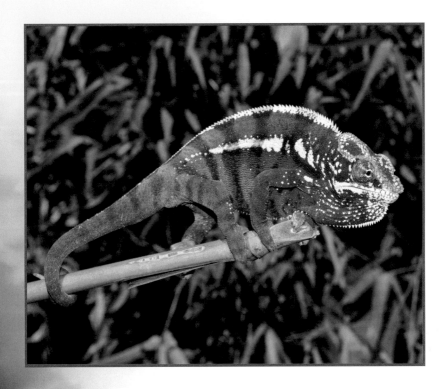

The chameleon can change colors in about 20 seconds.

The colors of some animals say "Stay away from me!"

These tiny frogs have **poison** in them.

Their bright
colors tell
other animals
"I taste bad!"

Other animals do not
eat the frogs.

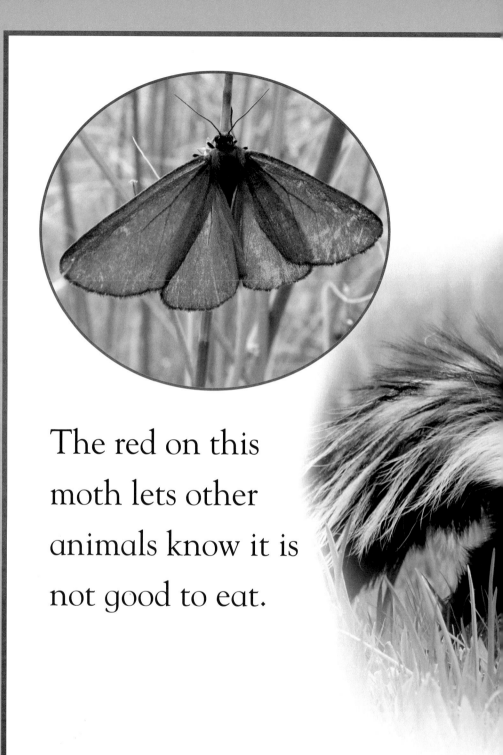

The red on this moth lets other animals know it is not good to eat.

A skunk's white stripes
say "Go away!"

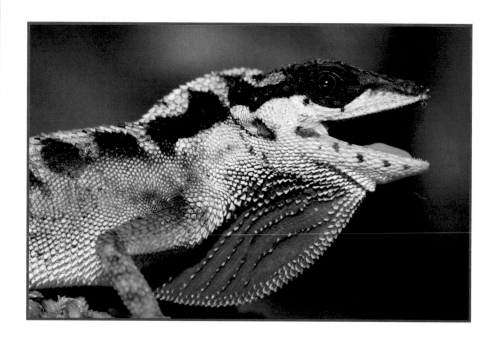

The colors of some animals
help them find **mates**.

This male lizard's orange neck
says "Here I am!"

The bright color helps
female lizards find him.

This male peacock has bright tail feathers.

Females look for males with the brightest feathers.

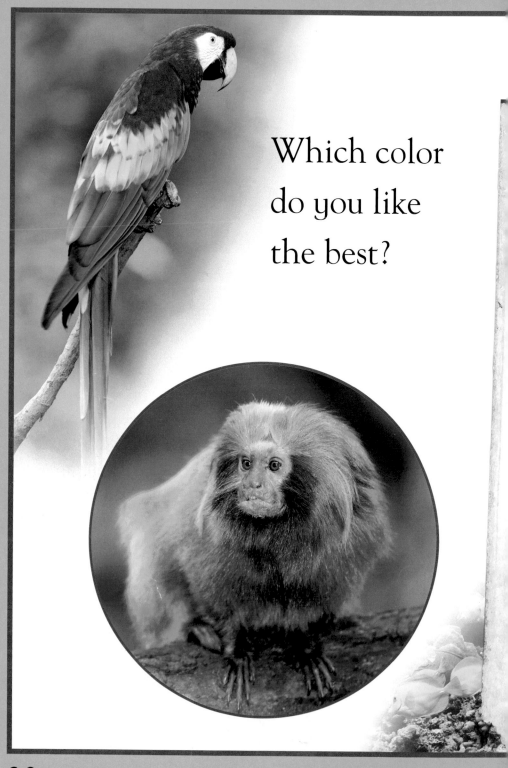

Which color
do you like
the best?

Do you see an animal
that color in this book?

Glossary

blend to mix in with other things of the same color and be hard to see, such as a brown hare in front of earth or rocks

camouflage when an animal's colors helps it hide from other animals

hare a furry animal with long ears that looks a lot like a rabbit

mate an animal that gets together with another animal to have babies

poison something that some animals make that can kill other animals

If you have enjoyed reading
this book, look out for more in
the Kingfisher Readers series!

**Collect
and read
them all!**

KINGFISHER READERS: LEVEL 1

Animal Colors ☐
Baby Animals ☐
Busy as a Bee ☐
Butterflies ☐
Colorful Coral Reefs ☐
Jobs People Do ☐
Seasons ☐
Snakes Alive! ☐
Tadpoles and Frogs ☐
Trains ☐
Tyrannosaurus! ☐

KINGFISHER READERS: LEVEL 2

Fur and Feathers ☐
In the Rainforest ☐
Trucks ☐
What Animals Eat ☐
Where Animals Live ☐
Where We Live ☐
Your Body ☐

For a full list of Kingfisher Readers books, plus
guidance for teachers and parents and activities
and fun stuff for kids, go to the Kingfisher Readers
website: www.kingfisherreaders.com